The Wise Up Challenge: Keys to Living A Wealthy, Successful and Fulfilling Life in Jesus Christ

By Chenelle B. Price

LEVE Publishing

ISBN: 978-0-9982391-0-1

Table of Contents

Preface

Proverbs 3:13-15 NLT

[13] Joyful is the person who finds wisdom,

the one who gains understanding.

[14] For wisdom is more profitable than silver,

and her wages are better than gold.

[15] Wisdom is more precious than rubies;

nothing you desire can compare with her.

Where would we be in a world without wisdom? What does the body of Christ, society, even our own individual lives look like without wisdom as a primary aspect? These are the questions I wonder if King

Solomon pondered on when he decided the best thing to ask God for was wisdom.

Wisdom is a strategized plan activated by applied knowledge. A world without it would be a world full of chaos, instability, irrational spontaneity, and destruction. It would be a world of missed opportunities, regret, broken relationships, and can even result in the increase and spread of many sicknesses and incurable illnesses; this can even result in death.

Gaining wisdom is the pathway to all wealth and success. There are some people who become financially wealthy overnight, but one thing that people must know is that wealth is not only based on one's financial stance, but wealth is also a mindset. Wealth is not only determined by material possessions, but by ideas and God-given knowledge and wisdom. When one begins to seek God for wisdom, they have then grabbed hold of the greatest key to wealth there is. Each and every one of us possesses a gift, a ministry, a purpose in us that has the potential to make us successful. Success doesn't always mean being a multi-millionaire, driving luxury cars, or even having a mega-ministry; success is fulfilling the purpose that God has predestined for your life. We are wealthy in ideas and pathways to help us reach this success; it is through the wisdom of God and much prayer and communication with Him that we are able to attain the keys to unlock what God has already placed inside of us. Deuteronomy 8:18a states *"But thou shalt remember the Lord thy God, for it is He that giveth thee power to get wealth...."*

When we seek the Lord, we gain all that we need to become successful believers in Christ. 1 Kings Chapter 3 talks about when Solomon asked the Lord for wisdom. We see in verses 12 and 13 that not only did God grant Solomon wisdom, but He also granted him *"riches and honor"* (vs.13). This coincides with what Jesus says in Matthew 6:33 *"But seek ye first the Kingdom of God, and His righteousness, and all these things shall be added unto you."*

Wise-Up was a term that many people used in the early 1990's. This term was slang for "get wisdom" or "use wisdom." Many times in our life we have been in a place where we should have "wised up" and chose not to. One major time that we see this type of situation is at the beginning of each year. Many people decide to make New Year Resolutions like becoming physically fit, or starting school, doing a bible plan, whatever their resolution may be, but often times they find that by mid-year they have slowly fallen off.

Godly wisdom helps us with everything we need to fulfill our tasks, even if it is time management or when to rest. As a child, I heard many of the adults around me use the phrase, "if I knew then what I know now"; this is something that can be prevented more if we seek out the wisdom of God and apply it to our life. If we took the time to apply godly wisdom, there would be a decrease in the amount of mistakes we make, and an increase in goals we complete.

Are you at a crossroads in your life? Have you lost sight of the plan God has for you? Are you at a place of instability, and have no idea what direction your life is heading? This devotional journal is designed to help you get back on track and become closer to gaining wisdom, wealth, and success in all areas of your life.

In the Wise-Up Challenge, we will touch on eight

major areas in which godly wisdom will help us become better in our life: Life Application, Spiritual, Mental, Financial, Emotional, Social, Educational, and Physical. If you have struggles in any of these areas, it is time for you to *"wise up!"* Feel free to use the extra pages after each section for notes, or to write prayers as an aid to help you improve in those areas.

When Opportunity Knocks

Ephesians 5:17 (NIV) "Therefore do not be foolish, but understand what the Lord's will is."

Are you an opportunist, or one who seeks the Lord for guidance? Every opportunity that is set before us is not from God. We often times find ourselves miserable on our jobs, in bad relationships, in the wrong crowd of people, lacking in finances, in the wrong lane in ministry etc. because we jumped on the first opportunity before us, or the one that *"appeared"* to be best, rather than seeking the Lord for His perfect will for our life. True enough, jumping into some of these opportunities may appear to be what is best in the natural, but what would the Holy Spirit have told us was the best action to take? What would have happened had we had applied godly wisdom and faith to our situation?

I can remember being at place in my life where rather than seeking the wisdom of God, I was desperate for a solution so I almost jumped on an opportunity that could have placed me at a point of setback. I had been working at a particular place of employment for about a year. I had finally gotten to a place where I was stable; I was no longer homeless and had just gotten a new car, was working towards furthering my education only to come to work on a Monday morning and find that by the end of the week, our company was going out of business and that I may have no longer had a job. My first instinct was to immediately start looking for more work and I did so. Within two days, I was hired at another company, but the Lord spoke to me as I was walking out of the job I was leaving on my last day and said, *"be still and know that I am God"* (Psalm 46:10). Hesitantly, I took heed to the word of the Lord, and after letting go of my fleshly thoughts I began to pray more and more about the situation, building my faith. By the end of the week, the Lord made it where another company took over our place of employment, in which not only did I receive an immediate raise, but after a few years I was promoted and placed on salary. In between that time, I had heard numerous complaints about the company I was going to move to, and thanked God for intervening before I made a

2

major mistake and placed myself in a position where I would have been stagnant. Little did I know, standing still would give me all of the necessary tools I needed to be catapulted into the next phase of my destiny years later. I could not imagine what would have happened had I made the move before me rather than waiting on the Most High and following His will.

In all things, we have to know that God knows what is best for us and will never lead us astray. The word tells is that "*He will sustain us*" (Psalm 55:22) so we never have to worry about jumping to and fro, putting ourselves at risk of missing our God-ordained opportunities and taking much longer than necessary to reach our destiny.

The wisest decision we can make in all situations is to seek the guidance of the Holy Spirit, rather than going on our own instincts and intuitions. This could lead us on a path to destruction and cause us to take on unnecessary challenges stemming from the choices we have made.

We also have to be careful when opportunities are before us because we never want to idolize an opportunity and put it in the place of our Father, making the

3

opportunity and what may come with it our new god. We will know that this is beginning to take place in our life when these things become more of a priority to us than God; when we begin to focus on those things first rather than our Lord. For example, if we begin to put more energy into our job, even in terms of timeliness and being on time for our secular job but late for the things of God, we are then prioritizing it before God. This is something we want to make sure never occurs in our life.

No matter how big or small the opportunity may appear to be, seek the Lord on which direction to go and what to do; even what appears to be the smallest of opportunities can have a major impact on our life.

Today's challenge is to write down some opportunities that are before you right now, or some goals in life that you want to achieve. Seek the Lord for His will and timing, allow Him to put it into action, and watch wealth and success begin to unfold in your life.

Application Prayer:

Heavenly Father,

Give me the wisdom and ability to discern opportunities that are for me and those which are not. I pray that doors that You have designated me to walk through be more appealing than those of the world, and that You help me make the right choices. Help me not to be so hasty and quick to take every opportunity that comes my way, but to hear Your voice and follow Your divine plan for my life.

I desire to have more trust in You and I pray that I am able to always remember that You have promised to sustain me in all things. Help me to never be deterred from following Your perfect will and help me not to idolize opportunities, so that they will never take Your place as my god. Let me never find more pleasure in opportunities, or the things that come with them than I find in You.

In Jesus' name, Amen.

Removing Negativity

Philippians 4:8 (GNT) "In conclusion, my friends, fill your minds with those things that are good and that deserve praise: things that are true, noble, right, pure, lovely, and honorable..."

In order for us to be positive people, we have to have positive thinking. Everything about the way we function begins in the mind. This is why the word tells us to think on things that are positive. It has been proven through research that the source of many illnesses is negativity and negative thinking. Negative thinking is one of the main causes of chronic stress and can cause your immune system to weaken, opening your body up to illness. This can also affect your blood pressure, hormone release, blood sugar, and many functions of the body.

One of the best ways to keep a positive mindset is to think on the goodness of the Lord! Everything that is good and perfect comes from the Most High. Psalm 145:3 says *"Great is the LORD! He is most worthy of praise! No one can measure his greatness."* Even when things don't look the best in our situations, if we have no other reason to be positive, this would be the greatest one! When we begin to praise the Lord for His greatness, we forget about every negative thing that could try to keep our mind in captivity, we are able to reach a point of breakthrough and peace, and our mind is renewed in the things of God.

When we read the word of God, we see David, who is running for his life from his charge King Saul, who was jealous of him and wanted to kill him. In the midst of a situation where fear, doubt, confusion and depression could have set it, he said in Psalm 34:

"I will bless the LORD at all times: his praise shall continually be in my mouth.

2 My soul shall make her boast in the LORD: the humble shall hear thereof, and be glad.

3 O magnify the LORD with me, and let us exalt his name together."

When we desire to have a more positive lifestyle, we also need to check our surroundings. We learn from Amos 3:3 that two can't walk together *"unless they agree."* What type of people are in your surroundings? Are they people who are pessimistic and always look for the worst? When you have a mindset of negative thoughts like *"I can't," "I won't"* or *"I don't have,"* you not only limit yourself, but you place a limit on what God is capable of doing in your life. Speaking life to yourself and your situations through faith causes a supernatural turn-around. Anything we believe we are capable of doing through Christ we can do (Philippians 4:13). We even see in the word that *"as a man thinks in his heart, so is he:"* (Proverbs 23:7), therefore, we should always think positive and speak life to ourselves.

Gossip is a major trap of the enemy that can not only have a person caught up in a bad situation, but it can cause negative thinking. When we allow people to talk to us about others, it can cause distortion in our mind concerning an individual and put us in a place where we find that we have an ought against that person formed by someone else. This creates unnecessary conflict in our life. In addition to the negativity it brings our way, we are then looked at as part of the problem in the eyesight of the Lord. Proverbs 17:4 tells us, *"An evildoer listens to wicked lips, and a liar gives ear to a mischievous tongue."*

Today's challenge is for you to think of ways to invite positivity into your life. What areas do you need to reduce negative thinking? What things in your life do you need to speak life to? How can you prevent yourself from having a negative mindset? What do you need to change about your surroundings?

Application Prayer:

Father,

I pray that I am able to think on things that are true, things that are just, things that are pure, things that are honest, lovely and of good rapport. I pray Lord that You would remove all negativity from my mind, heart and spirit. Help me to have a more positive view of myself and every situation I encounter. Though hardships may occur in life that may be difficult to deal with, I pray that You give me a heart that is able to give thanks in all circumstances.

Surround me with people who will make spiritual deposits in my life that will help me become better and think positive. Help me to speak life to every negative situation and remove people from my life that mean me no good. Today, I decree that I "can't, won't" or "am not capable of" are removed from my vocabulary, and I speak that I can do all things through You that strengthens me! Tame my tongue and help me to refrain from gossip as well as engaging through listening.

These requests I render in Your Son Jesus' name, Amen!
11

Be Who God Designed You to Be!

Isaiah 64:8 "But now, O LORD,
thou art our father; we are the clay,
and thou our potter; and we
all are the work of thy hand."

It is amazing to think that among the countless
wonders we see in the world- the mountains, hills,
animals, plants, even the seas, that we are one of the
creations God placed on the potter's wheel. The Lord
spoke to the prophet Jeremiah in the first chapter and
said, *"Before I formed thee in the belly, I knew thee"*
(Jeremiah 1:5a). Isn't it a blessing to know that we serve
a God who loves us so dearly that before He even placed
us in the earth He had already paved our life path and had
blessings in store for us? Before God formed us in our
mother's womb, He predestined us and had in mind our
assignment, our gifting…our destiny. This means what

13

once we entered this earth, we began the journey to finding out who God wants us to be, and what He wants us to do. Once we have reached the place where we know our identity in Him, it is our responsibility to gain everything we need from the Lord to cultivate what He has placed in us.

Often times, there are people in the body of Christ who lose sight of who God has crafted them to be. They sometimes find that they are more comfortable doing something else; maybe operating in another gift looks easier, more appealing, or may appear to be more substantial or popular. These are the wiles of the enemy that blind-sight us and cause us to miss out on what God has for us. We can never reach our highest potential without submitting to the will of God, and being who He wants us to be. You must learn to fully surrender to the will of God and "be uniquely who you were called and created to be." (Apostle Warren Curry).

How would you feel if you put so much thought into a gift you planned on giving someone on a special occasion and they rejected it? This is the way God feels when we reject what He has placed inside of us, to pursue something we presume is greater. We see in the book of Romans where the Apostle Paul states, *"But indeed, O man, who are you to reply against God? Will the thing formed say to him who formed it, "Why have you made me like this?"* (Romans 9:20). When God formed us, He knew our life-task and equipped us with what we needed to fulfill it. When we make an attempt to take a form contrary to what God designed us to be, we will find that we are not equipped with the tools necessary to fulfill *that* plan, because it is not the plan God had for us. Imagine an electrician attempting to complete a task meant for someone who is an expert in plumbing; though they may have a slight idea on how to complete the task, they would not have the necessary tools to complete it, and may not even know all that is necessary to fix the problem, as their expertise is electrical work. This is similar to what we experience when we try to fulfill a purpose we were not assigned by God to fulfill. We will also find that we have been sidetracked from reaching our destiny and it causes a delay to our spiritual promotion.

In ministry, we find some people who are not content with being Teachers, Evangelists, or even

15

Worship Leaders, but want to be Bishops, Prophets and Apostles; attempting to walk in the position without the mantle. There is no way to find spiritual stability if you are in the wrong lane. Everyone is not created to do the same thing, and there is no gift that is greater than another. Whatever God has placed in you to do, *"do it heartily, as to the Lord, and not unto men; Knowing that of the Lord ye shall receive the reward of the inheritance: for ye serve the Lord Christ."* (Colossians 3:23-24 KJV)! When we think about the fact that the gift God has placed in us is being used for Him and not for ourselves or for men, then we have a better appreciation for it and will have the mindset to do all we can to make sure that every task within it is carried out in excellence. When we learn to appreciate our gifts, we find that we do not need to search for our call in other areas, or allow people to tell us what we are supposed to be doing in God's Kingdom.

We as believers in Christ have to remember that above all, we are called to *serve*. When we make this our top priority, we then see the big picture and how the many members of this one body spoken of in Romans

Chapter 12 come together and serve the great purpose of glorifying our Father.

What is the gift God has given you? What can you do to make sure you are doing your part to make sure the body is functioning? How confident are you in the gift God has given you? How can you make sure to cultivate your gifts?

I challenge you today whether you are a Worship Leader, Dancer, Singer, Minister, Pastor, Bishop, Intercessor, or even just one who serves the Lord with your heart, to appreciate the call that God has placed on your life, and do all you can to take it to the fullest potential.

Application Prayer:

Dear Lord,

Today I have decided to become all You have designed me to be. No longer will I try to do things my way, or be someone other than who You called me to be. I repent for any way I may have tried to reconstruct Your plan for my life, knowingly or unknowingly. You are the potter and I am the clay...shape me to be used for Your glory! I pray that I reach my fullest potential in You and that everything I do will be pleasing in Your sight. Help me not to become blind-sighted by giftings, ministries and/or opportunities that "appear" to be more appealing to me. Give me an unchangeable appreciation for what You have called me to do, and help me to do it heartily as unto You and not unto men. Help me to both understand and embrace the role I play in the body of Christ as well as in my home or work environment.

In Jesus' name, Amen.

Wonderful, Incredible You...

Psalm 139:14-15 "Oh yes, you
shaped me first inside, then out; you
formed me in my mother's womb. I
thank you, High God—you're
breathtaking! Body and soul, I am
marvelously made! I worship in
adoration—what a creation! You
know me inside and out, you know
every bone in my body, You know
exactly how I was made, bit by
bit, how I was sculpted from nothing
into something."

One of the most fascinating gifts that has ever been given is the gift of life. This is something special that only God can give; something He gave to each and every one of us. God thought so much of us that He gave us life, and still expresses His love toward us though His son, Jesus Christ who gave his life as ransom for us on the cross.

When God created us, He thought out every detail strategically! He wanted to assure that we were all created in His image and His likeness as the word defines us in the book of Genesis. This means that every great quality that we have was inspired by God's own character.

It is a ploy of the enemy to make us feel like we are not God's great creation; he wants us to feel that we don't look good enough, aren't smart enough, don't make enough money, and can never amount to what God wants us to, or anything else. When God created most parts of the earth and its inhabitants as we see in the book of Genesis, He said *"it was good."* When we look at the day He created man, He said that "it was *very* good" (Genesis 1:31). This leads me to believe that we, man, me, you are seen as one of God's greatest creations! Therefore we should make every attempt to see ourselves as God sees us, and love ourselves as He does. When we learn to see ourselves the way God does, we then get to a place where we esteem ourselves better, yet remaining humble and praising God as King David did in Psalm 139.

21

We should never allow Satan to attack our mind concerning our self-esteem. Everyone was created uniquely, yet in the image of God. When we allow Satan to diminish our self-esteem, we then open the door for him to reap havoc in our life. Having low self-esteem can invite depression, suicidal thoughts, under or over-eating and more into our lives. It can even put us in a place where we allow people into our life that are not good for us. There are many people who have allowed people to come into their life and take advantage of them due to having low self-esteem. There are also people who are in abusive relationships where the root is low self-esteem. These type relationships are also rooted in fear, and can even be rooted in rejection. If we feel like we are nothing, then it makes Satan feel as if he has the power to overtake us. John 10:10 tells us that he only comes to *"steal, kill, and destroy."* When we get to that place where we truly believe that we are fearfully and wonderfully made, we activate the power God placed in us during our stage of creation, and can defeat the enemy in our lives!

Every day that you call yourself ugly, you are calling God a liar, who said His creation was very good. Every time you put yourself down or speak negatively about yourself or your capabilities, you are speaking negatively about the work of God. *"Death and life are in the power of the tongue."* (Proverbs 18:21).

Look in the mirror every morning and say something positive about yourself, and thank God for it. If you have a problem with what you see in the mirror, start with one of your facial-features or something you like about your body. Thank God for some of the characteristics you have and begin creating a pathway to freedom. The more you begin encouraging yourself, the more you will see what you say. It may not be easy to do at first, and you may not even fully believe what you say, but don't give up. What do you like most about your body? What is your favorite feature? What is your favorite characteristic about yourself? How can you use something about your characteristics to praise God? What steps do you need to make to better love yourself? I challenge you today to encourage yourself each day so that you see yourself as God sees you!

Application Prayer:

Father,

Knowing that before You formed me in my mother's womb you knew me, I pray that I embrace the person You have made me. Your word says that I am fearfully and wonderfully made and I pray that I am able to see all that makes me such. Today, I commit to taking ownership of who I am and freely being the person You have created me to be; in Your image and likeness. I will speak positive and affirming words into my spirit, and surround myself with people who build me up rather than tearing me down. No longer will I put myself down, or allow others to put me down....no longer will I look in the mirror and despise what I see, but I will give thanks for every unique way You have made me. I commit to no longer comparing my body to others, to comparing my personality, my accomplishments or any other part of my life to anyone else. You have a perfect plan and will for my life, and according to Your pace, I will reach every goal You have set for me. I will not allow negative thoughts, thoughts of low self-esteem, or even thoughts of suicide have dominion over me. Help me to better love myself so that I am able to love others. Help me to see myself as You see me in every way; the things You love about me, and the things I need to change to become more aligned with Your likeness. Thank You Lord for loving me, for making me unique and for the new refreshing I will feel on this journey of loving and empowering myself.

In Jesus' name, Amen!

Grow Up!

---

1 Corinthians 13:11- "[11] When I was
a child, I spake as a child, I
understood as a child, I thought as a
child: but when I became a man, I put
away childish things."

When dealing with the issues of life, there comes a time where we have to mature in Christ. Lacking spiritual maturity results in continuing to practice old habits and addictions, as well as old ways of thinking. When we put away our carnal way of thinking, we begin to mature in Christ and grow to be the vessel God has predestined us to be.

In the scripture, the Apostle Paul first talks about how when he was a child, he spoke as a child. One of the conclusions that can be drawn when thinking of children and their communication is that they do not always think before they speak. Sometimes, the things children say may be true, but their delivery may not come off very pleasing to some people. This is something people in the body of Christ should be mindful of as well. There are times where what we may have to say may be true, but it's our delivery that makes the difference in whether our point is accepted or rejected by most people. We have to make sure that the love of Christ is displayed, no matter what comes out of our mouth.

Paul also talks about how he understood as a child. Children often times go off what they see before them. They have a very difficult time seeing beyond their present situation. This also happens in the body of Christ when we lack faith. We only look at the bills we see on the table, the rapport the doctor gave us, the deadlines we may have, the reactions of the people around us, but we don't always take the time to stop and gain sight beyond sight through the Holy Spirit.

When we are not spiritually mature, we think as a child as well. Children often have the mindset "my way or the highway." For example, if a child is in the grocery store with their parent, and see a chocolate bar, if they ask for it and the parent says "no" or "wait," they may throw a tantrum. There are people in the body of Christ who walk in spiritual immaturity who will do the same thing. If they want that new car or job, if they want to hit the lottery, that guy or girl they like who may look perfect for them, but if they don't receive those things, they will throw a tantrum. These are the type people who decide because God didn't move on their terms, they aren't going to sow into the ministry, they're going to stop their work for the kingdom, and they may even stop coming to church altogether. These are the people who get angry at the Lord and talk about how much He hates them when in actuality, they are the ones who may be harboring that very feeling towards God.

Paul goes on to say in his scripture *"but when I became a man, I put away childish things."* When we decide to put away our ways of spiritual immaturity, we then open ourselves up to be more used by God. There are many in the body of Christ who are being used, but are not being used to their fullest capacity because they refuse to feed their spirit and give it the proper nourishment to grow. Proper nourishment for our spirit is reading the word of God, allowing it to penetrate our heart, remaining in constant communication with the Lord, praying and fasting and so much more! When we become mature spiritually, we have then positioned our minds to receive deeper revelations from God that will not only help us spiritually, but in all areas of our life.

Spiritual maturity means that you have allowed God to groom you and make you more aligned to His likeness. When one lacks spiritual maturity, it is evident in all they do and flows out into other parts of their life. You will see that many of their actions do not line up to the things that define God and having His likeness.

We have to make sure we remember that natural age does not define spiritual maturity! Having this misconception can prevent spiritual growth. This is something that is seen often in the body of Christ.

There are many people who have been in church their entire lives, who do not grow because they feel that the years they have spent in the church determines their growth, rather than how much they have learned and applied. There are people who are considered our elders who are still "babes in Christ," because they are unwilling to learn or change, holding the mindset that they know more because they have been in church longer, or having the mindset that a person younger in age can't enlighten them in the word.

There are various places in the word of God where we see people who were both young and wise, as well as people who were *older* and foolish. We see Josiah, who became king at 8 years old and served the Lord, but we also see King Hezekiah, who in his more mature physical age made foolish decisions and had to be granted 15 more years of life by God.

What ways will you make sure you are casting down spiritual immaturity? How will you make sure not to turn back to a carnal mindset? I encourage you to ask God to show you the areas in your life where you need to mature, and allow Him to begin the spiritual makeover process so that your spiritual maturity flows from the inside out.

Application Prayer:

Heavenly Father,

I am asking that You help me to mature in all areas of my life both in the natural and supernatural. Change my way of thinking and every action that may be immature. Help me to self-examine and reflect on ways that I can become better at all I do and more mature both in the natural realm as well as the spiritual. Perform a spiritual makeover to where the old me is no longer recognizable…to where I have become a better person in You. Help me to wait on You and have a more Christ-like understanding in all situations and circumstances. I pray that you would help me get to a place where I can be used even greater for Your glory.

In the name of Jesus, Amen.

Checking Our Love Walk

---

1 Corinthians 13:1-3 NIV "If I speak in the tongues of men or of angels, but do not have love, I am only a resounding gong or a clanging cymbal. ² If I have the gift of prophecy and can fathom all mysteries and all knowledge, and if I have a faith that can move mountains, but do not have love, I am nothing. ³ If I give all I possess to the poor and give over my body to hardship that I may boast, but do not have love, I gain nothing."

What does it take to love? This question can be simply answered: A heart that is willing. Having a heart that is willing to love means loving with the heart of God and not your own. When we as carnal people try to love with our own heart, we fail every time. Though the love that we give has different measures depending on the type and person, it is still love that is conditional. But when we love with the heart of God, we are able to love even our enemies. We have to be spiritually in tune with God to even love God unconditionally.

Situations may occur in our life where the love we have for God will be tested. There are times in our life where we want something so bad, and it does not happen for us. What do we do? Instantly, for some people, their heart turns to stone and they become angry at God. The longer that anger lies dormant, it becomes so deeply rooted that it becomes hatred. If they are not careful, this hatred can even become a false form of disbelief in God altogether.

I believe that many of the Atheists we see in the world today are not Atheists at all, but rather people who have allowed their heart to take a bitter form towards God because something tragic happened or something did not exactly go the way they thought it would in their life. This is because they have not stayed in the presence of

God long enough that their spirit has become intertwined with His. If our desires are lined up with God's, there would be no room for disappointment, which leaves no room for anger towards Him, or hate. We have to learn to love God with our all so that when the enemy tries to attack our mind, we are so in tune with His spirit that Satan won't succeed.

Checking our love walk requires a true desire to see what God wants to show us. Many of us say *"I want God to show me my heart,"* but when He begins to do so, we turn away and no longer want to see. Having a true desire to see what God sees will encourage us to press through and continue to watch as God reveals even the ugliest things in the depths of our hearts.

After acknowledging what God has shown us, then the real love walk can begin. How much do we love God? The bible tells us in John 14:15 that if we love Him, we will keep His commandments. True love towards God is being willing to let go of the things that displease God *totally*. Not being willing to totally let go of the things that displease God is like committing adultery. We as the church are "the bride of Christ" (Ephesians 5:23-24) and when we continuously commit sin, we are placing our loyalty with the enemy, similar to when infidelity is found in a natural marriage. When we decide to let go of sin, we are showing our full commitment, loyalty, and true love for God. The best thing about this is, God helps us through the process!

Being created in the image and likeness of God (Genesis 1:26-27) is one reason we should love ourselves. If we find no other reason to love ourselves, we should because God has shared pieces of the many attributes He has with us when He formed us in our mother's womb! If we have no love for ourselves, how much more will we love someone else, whom God has also made? Loving ourselves and loving God teaches us to appreciate how God has made us and what He has equipped us with enough to look deep inside and see how we can use the precious gifts God put in us to help someone else.

How much do you love your neighbor? There are two things that we see in both the Old and New Testament that never change; the fact that the bible tells us to love God with all of our heart, soul, might and mind, and to love our neighbor as we love ourselves

(Deuteronomy 6:5, Leviticus 19:18, Luke 10:27). The best thing we can do is love with our all, as Jesus did when he died on the cross for us. Despite our imperfections, Jesus still displayed unconditional love toward us; unconditional meaning as wide as it is deep. What I mean by this is that our love unconditional should always remain-it should be never-ending.

The word of God says that *"love covers a multitude of sin"* (1 Peter 4:8)*, and the same love that Christ used to cast our transgression *"as far as the east is from the west"* (Psalm 103:12), this is the same love we are expected to show to our brother and sister when they offend us. God accepts us every day; even with our sin He loves us, yet one of the most difficult things for man to do is love someone past the things that make them far from perfect. This is the reason we should go the extra mile to love our enemies or those who hurt us. When we love with the heart of God, withholding love from anyone is impossible.

Are you showing the love of Christ to others on a daily basis? How far do you go to show love to those it may be challenging to deal with? I challenge you today to write down a few ways you can spread love to the people you encounter every day. Make a phone call, send an email or message, leave someone a voicemail, mend a relationship, do what you have to do to love someone today; do what is necessary to love yourself today and most of all, do what you have to do to show love to Christ today!

Application Prayer:

Lord,

I want to express my love to You more…teach me Your ways that I may express my love towards You by keeping Your commandments as Your word says. I pray that You touch my heart and help me love others and myself with Your heart, a heart that is pure and not my own, one which is carnal. I pray that through loving with Your heart I am able to love others even when it may be difficult…when it may be painful, with the same unconditional love You showed me when You sent Your Son to die on the cross for my sins. Today, I choose to let go of any anger, unforgiveness and bitterness that may keep me from loving with Your love. Heal my heart from all pain I have experienced, that I may be able to move forward today walking in Your love and Spirit.

In Jesus' name, Amen.

Integrity, Integrity, INTEGRITY!

Proverbs 10:9 ESV- "Whoever walks
in integrity walks securely, but he who
makes his ways crooked will be found
out."

One of the wisest things we can do for ourselves as
people is walk in integrity. Walking in integrity means
that we are constantly walking in truth and doing things
according to God's plan, rather than following the
mischievous plan of the enemy. To walk in integrity also
means to do what is righteous in the eyes of God, even
behind closed doors. We have to be mindful that as
believers in Christ, we are *"living epistles"* (2 Corinthians
3:2); we are the story of who Christ is to many, therefore
we have to do our best to exemplify Christ through our
lifestyle and make sure He is being glorified. When we
share Christ with others, we should be able to use our
lifestyle to back up what we are saying.

42

When we look at the word of God, we learn that from John 10:10 that the enemy comes to *"steal, kill, and destroy."* If he can come up against our character and demolish it, he has gotten one step closer to building on to his kingdom by causing us to lose our witness and potential to win souls for the Kingdom of God. True enough, there will be people who may lie and diminish your character through their lies, but the word tells us what Jesus is the truth, and us being Kingdom believers in Christ, the truth will eventually be illuminated. When we walk in integrity, who we are will always overshadow who people say we are.

When we look in the book of Acts, one of the qualifications of the men chosen to help with Kingdom work was that they had to have a good rapport (Acts 6:3). As people of God, we have to have a reputation that is honorable and honest. When people see us, they should be able to see the fruit of the spirit (Galatians 5:22-23); they should be able to see the Spirit of God (Isaiah 11:2). Even Jesus himself in the prayer he prayed before the cross, asked that God would be glorified in him. When we walk in integrity, Christ is glorified in us, and there is

43

no mistake of his reign in our life. This is what the scripture means in Proverbs 10:9a where it says *"Whoever walks in integrity walks securely…"* The security we get from walking in integrity is even when people try to lie on us and slander our name, attack our character or challenge our integrity, the fruit we have produced and the evidence of the Holy Spirit living inside of us holds us securely to the rapport that we have in the Kingdom of God rather than the rapport man tries to build for us. God will not allow His kingdom to be made into a mockery, therefore referring back to Proverbs, anything indecent will be exposed, whether to the individual personally, or whether through public exposure; dishonestly will be brought to the forefront at all costs. God does this so that we can take a look in the mirror and rid ourselves of all sin or anything that will keep us from reaching the goals God has set for us. He wants us to walk in truth, so that we can lead others to truth.

In 1 Thessalonians 5:22, the Apostle Paul states that we should *"avoid the appearance of evil."* In this text, he is talking about ways to follow the expectations of God and how to be ready for the second coming of Christ. In any situation, we should make sure that we are not engaging in, or even have the appearance that we are engaging in any activity that challenges our integrity.

Even as honest people, there will come times where we will make mistakes, but what should we do? Well, the Holy Spirit expects us to first acknowledge them (Proverbs 28:13). One of the easiest ways to fall back into our same issues is to sweep them under the rug. We then must repent, turn away, and use our mistakes as a learning experience for growth. Depending on what issue we may have, we may even need an accountability partner to help keep us remain focused and walking in integrity. This is not to say that we should talk to *everyone* about our issues or struggles, but it may require us to seek the Holy Spirit to help us find someone trustworthy, who is willing to labor in prayer on our behalf and keep us on track as we walk through the journey of fixing our mistakes (James 5:16). Making these attempts towards improvement shows great integrity because not only are we being true to God, but we are being true to ourselves and our spiritual walk.

What things can you do to assure that you are walking in a lifestyle that displays integrity? How can you assure that you remain honest in all situations? I challenge you to do some self-examination. Write down some things about yourself that need a tune-up. Write some things that you want God to move out of the way so that you can walk out a life of total integrity.

Application Prayer:

Heavenly Father,

I pray that you would help me live a lifestyle that is holy and pleasing unto You...help me to live a life of integrity, even when others cannot see...I understand that you have made me a living epistle and that people are watching how I live for You....be glorified though my lifestyle, from the words that come out of my mouth, to my actions and the way I treat others. Give me the boldness to hold my friends and loved ones accountable to the same expectation You have set for me, to walk in integrity and live as an example of Your greatness.
In Jesus' name, Amen.

Fully Faithful

Matthew 25:23 (KJV) - "His lord
said unto him, Well done, good and
faithful servant; thou hast been
faithful over a few things, I will make
thee ruler over many things: enter
thou into the joy of thy lord."

How often have you looked at your possessions and felt like they were not enough? Have you looked at your business, your ministry, your organization and felt perplexed wondering why it isn't growing or prospering? When these type of situations arise, the first thing we should check is how faithful we have been over these things.

While driving on the road one day, Bishop Victor Couzens came on the radio and was talking about vision and destiny. One of the things he stated that stuck with me was "It's God's vision, we are just the stewards of it…" I sat in the parking lot outside of my church and began thinking deeply on what I had just heard. *Are we good stewards of the vision of God? What does a good steward look like?*

Being a good steward over anything God gives us will show great faithfulness and dedication. A good steward of God's vision is one who is humble enough to remember that the vision belongs to God, but is committed enough to steward the vision as if it is their own. When we continue to acknowledge the fact that the vision we are responsible for belongs to God, we create a blockade that prevents the spirit of pride from taking precedence in our spirit. Once we try to take the position that belongs to the Creator, we set ourselves up for destruction, not to mention the fact that we show God that we are not responsible enough to care for His vision or ministry.

One who is good in stewardship of the vision God has placed in their care works diligently regardless of how much extra help they may have. These people

49

understand that even if everyone else walks away, because the vision or ministry was placed in their hands, they are responsible for keeping it alive.

Another example of stewardship is making investments. When God trusts us with a vision, the expectation is that we make an investment that will be beneficial and help push that vision forward. The same is with a business or even a ministry. We must use godly wisdom and make investments that will bring forth fruitful results. A great example in the word of God comes from Matthew 25:14-30. In this parable, there were servants that were given different amounts of gold. I personally believe that the master gave them varied amounts based upon what he thought they could handle. For the ones who invested their gold, they saw the manifestation and were told by the master that they would receive an abundance because they were able to show the fruit of their investments. One of the servants chose to hide his bag of gold rather than invest it, and was scolded in return. Choosing not to invest what God has entrusted us with causes our role in Kingdom advancing to become stagnant, but we when make positive investments, we see positive results and receive blessings from our Father.

God expects us to be good stewards over the body He has given us. True enough, our body will not go with us when our life is completed here on earth, but while we are here, we must take care of our body so that our time is enjoyable and not filled with miscellaneous health issues that could be prevented by eating right and exercising. When we are good stewards over our body by eating the right foods, exercising and getting the proper rest, we feel more energized and can do much more than if we are not taking care of ourselves. God wants us to be in *"good health"* (3 John 1:2). When we don't take our health into account, we open ourselves up for the enemy to inflict sicknesses on us, making our life here on earth more difficult than it has to be.

In addition to not eating the right foods, resting, or exercising, refraining from substance abuse plays a role in the stewardship of our body as well. We must make sure we are not defiling our body by consuming things that can be harmful to us. When we take in things like nicotine, drugs and alcohol, we defile our body by consuming substances that can be poisonous and eventually cause problems for us physically. These problems include various diseases, infections and even cancer.

Making sure to rest properly, eating healthy, and exercising are great ways of assuring that your body is as healthy as your spirit-man is when you feed the word of God to your spirit.

Parenting is another one of the areas in which God expects us to be good stewards. For each and every one of God's children, He has a purpose and plan, and it is the responsibility of earthly parents to cultivate the gifts inside of the children and help them walk out their purpose. It is every parent's responsibility, mother and father, to make lifelong investments into their children. The starting point of being good stewards of God's children is showing them love and giving them the care that is necessary to help them grow and develop. When parents begin to see their role as steward over their child as a blessing more than a responsibility, they are motivated to invest more time, money and energy into helping them become the best they can be. We must teach children about investing by caring for them when they are young so that they care for us when we are old. Our children should never get to a place where they feel they are not loved. We are responsible for expressing the love of Christ to them, and teaching them how to express that same love to others.

Investing and instilling the principles of love is the same as instilling the principles of God; God is love (1 John 4:16)! Doing this will bring forth more positive results in the world we live in today. This is the key to reducing the amount of violence, racism and other forms of negativity we see in our world. We have to teach and train them on how to be future men and women of God, and how to be good stewards of their gifts God has entrusted them with as well. If this is done, it will become an on-going cycle of investment and manifestation of gifts, ministries, businesses, organizations, programs and people all created to give glory to God. These same principles can be applied in marriage as well as other relationships.

In marriage, the end result of applying these principals are love, joy and longevity. God never intended for marriage to be something that was temporary. In the days of Adam and Eve, we read in the word of God that Eve was formed from the rib of Adam and after that, there was no other woman that was made for Adam. True enough, there are trials that would come with any marriage or relationship, and thinking about the scenario from the Garden of Eden, we can only wonder what happened after, but we never read that Adam and Eve separated after the garden incident; they had to work through things together.

It was love and dedication that took Mary to the manger where our Savior was born. Though in between a rock and hard place, where Joseph could have left Mary after hearing of her pregnancy and even considered quietly dismissing her, he trusted the word from God and stayed with Mary every step of the way. This shows true faithfulness! When we are faithful to relationships, whether with friends or family, displaying godly love and abiding by God's principles will bear continuous fruit.

Take some time to do some reflection: What areas do you need to become more faithful? How can you be a better steward over your business, ministry, or even in relationships? It's time to wise up and be fully faithful in every way possible so that God can say *"Well done, good and faithful servant; thou hast been faithful over a few things, I will make thee ruler over many things"* Matthew 25:23.

Application Prayer:

Heavenly Father,

Help me to become more faithful in everything I do...show me what areas in my life lack faithfulness and help me to become more dedicated in my words and actions. Today, I am deciding to work on becoming more faithful to my marriage, my children and my family. I commit to taking my responsibilities more serious and being a better steward in every position I hold, whether in ministry, in my household or on my job. I understand that You have entrusted me with blessings that I am to invest into and bring forth productivity. Today, I commit to taking better care of my body by eating the right foods, exercising, making rest a priority, and seeking help to remove any addictions I may have from my life that could potentially harm me. I thank You for giving me this opportunity to make a change for the better and to reverse any negative results of lacking faithfulness before it is too late.

Today, I even take the time to recommit myself to You, as my Lord and personal Savior and will work diligently to advance Your Kingdom.

In Jesus' name, Amen!

Forgive and Forget?

Ephesians 4:32 (ESV) "Be kind to one another, tenderhearted, forgiving one another, as God in Christ forgave you."

One of the biggest issues people seem to have in life is harboring unforgiveness. There have been people who have been hurt in their childhood and have carried those issues into their adulthood... there are people who have said things to others in the body of Christ, causing one to stray away and use this as a reason why they do not gather with other believers or have a "church-home" and there are families that remain severed over words that have been spoken by family members or painful actions that have been displayed. There are even people who go to work and refuse to say a word to their co-workers because of something that was said to them, or friendships that have been broken all due to the spirit of unforgiveness.

Often times we hear people say "we must forgive and forget." On the flip side, we hear others saying "it's ok to forgive, but never forget what the person has done to you"…which is the correct way of thinking? Let's look at the example given in the word of God. When we look at the Old Testament, the children of Israel were constantly sinning against God. The Lord always made promises to them, told them how much He loved them, yet they still chose to straddle the fence in serving God in one season, and turning their backs on Him the next. This hurt God, but throughout the Old Testament we see many prophets who spoke a word to them of God's wrath and even some punishment that they had inflicted upon themselves, but we also see God still offering promises to His chosen people. Furthermore, in the word of God, we see that He promises to forgive our wickedness and will remember our sins no more (Hebrews 8:12). This shows us that when God forgives us of sin, He forgets about it. Should we not do the same as God does by forgiving those who trespass against us then forgetting about it?

59

We have to beware that one of the results of harboring unforgiveness is carrying the issues into future relationships. There have been many relationships that did not work out between men and women due to someone being hurt in a past relationship and carrying their issues into the new relationship. There are some women who carry the mentality "all men are the same," therefore they ruin their next relationship because rather than spending the time building on the relationship they are establishing with their significant other, they find themselves consumed with trying to prove that it is "too good to be true" or that the person is just like every other man they have encountered.

Men also have this same issue-there are some men who have been hurt in past relationships and rather than opening their heart to the new woman they have encountered, they keep their guards up and some men even have other women just in case that one doesn't work out to save themselves from heartache. Not just in dealing with significant others, but in all relationships, we have to lose the "guilty until proven innocent" mentality. In every relationship we encounter, we should look at as Christ has viewed our relationship with him. God knew that we had flaws, which is why He sent Jesus to die on the cross for us. When we have chosen to forgive, we should be prepared to forget what the person has done to us. When dealing with other people, we should follow the word of God's instructions and *"let this mind be in us, which is also in Christ Jesus"* (Philippians 2:5); we must be prepared to love as Christ loves, forgive as Christ forgives, and forget as Christ forgets.

Another issue that arises concerning forgiveness is forgiving ourselves. Sometimes, we make mistakes in our life that put us in a place where we have a hard time forgiving our own self. The best way to deal with this is to *LET IT GO*! Romans 8:1 tells us that there is no condemnation for those who walk in Christ, so if Christ does not condemn us, who are we to condemn ourselves? Once we have made a decision to do better after learning from our mistakes, the expectation from God is for us to move forward, even if there are consequences attached to whatever decision we have made.

When we set our mind on the positive and move towards growing from the lesson learned from our mistakes rather than dwelling on our mistakes, we then prepare for a brighter future ahead and turn our mistake into a testimony of how God transformed both us and our situation.

Take the time to think back and reflect on all of those who have offended or hurt you, even since childhood. Write down the names of those people, and how they offended or hurt you. Activate the spirit of God within you by speaking to those situations and declaring that you have forgiven those people and surrendered to God to make you whole. Next, take the time to reflect even deeper: *Did you perform any initial actions to hurt that person or in retaliation for what they had done to hurt or offend you?* Pray and ask the Holy Spirit to guide you through asking for forgiveness from those people if you are able to reach out to them and to prepare you for whatever their response may be. *Disclaimer:* Because people are on different spiritual levels, and because some of the people you may be dealing with may not have a relationship with Jesus at all, there is a chance that your apology may not be accepted. This is why it is important to pray that the Holy Spirit prepares your heart in such a way that you are able to work through any feelings that may come if someone chooses not to accept your apology. Even in that situation, give thanks to God that He has worked on your heart in such a way that you were able to do what He expects and offer peace and reconciliation to that individual. Pray that godly relationships be renewed, and that peace resides in every situation!

Application Prayer:

Heavenly Father,

Please help me to have a heart that forgives and does not condemn others or myself. I pray that You would soften every hardened place in my heart and constantly remind me that in order to be forgiven, I have to forgive. I release any feelings I have that are attached to unforgiveness, any hatred, anger, resentment or bitterness...fill me with Your peace that passes all understanding, and prepare me for any response I may

receive when I go to those whom I have offended or hurt
on behalf of my own forgiveness. I pray that You would
mend relationships ordained by You, and bring
reconciliation even between me and those who are not
meant to have a permanent place in my life, that I may
walk in liberty and not carry unnecessary weight from
ungodly feelings. Help me to grow from my mistakes
rather than hold them against myself; help me to share
the testimony of where I am now and how I have evolved
from who I used to be.

In the name of Jesus, Amen!

Don't Worry

Philippians 4:6-7 NLT
"Don't worry about anything;
instead, pray about everything. Tell
God what you need, and thank him for
all he has done. 7 Then you will
experience God's peace, which
exceeds anything we can understand.
His peace will guard your hearts and
minds as you live in Christ Jesus."

So often, we find ourselves worrying about so many things- finances, our families, bills and expenses, our education, things that lead us to try to take matters into our own hands. How does God feel about this? Well, there are two words that the bible states in regards to worry- those words are *"fret not."* The word of God specifically instructs us not to worry about anything, because our Father in Heaven will take care of us.

In Matthew Chapter 6, Jesus assures us of God's care by reminding us that God knows all of our needs and will take care of our present day needs as well as our future needs. He also tells us to *"seek ye first the Kingdom of God, and His righteousness, and all these things shall be added unto you"* (Matthew 6:33 KJV). We must always remember that if we are following godly principles and listening for His direction, God will take care of our needs. God promises us that He will supply all of our needs *"according to his riches in glory by Christ Jesus"* (Philippians 4:19). We know that in the Lord's house there are many mansions and that God is filled with riches and honor, therefore there is nothing that is inaccessible to us when we obey God; we never have to worry about anything. Because God is our shepherd, we never have to want for anything because He promised us in His word that He would take care of us!

Have you ever looked around and seen someone in the world who may appear to be prospering while you are struggling? There are times where believers in Christ may begin to think this way; this is a tactic of the enemy in attempt to make believers feel as if they are not prospering or as if following the enemy's path is more beneficial. Psalm 37 is a great reminder to us that things are not as they appear. It begins with:

"¹Do not fret because of evildoers,
Nor be envious of the workers of iniquity.
²For they shall soon be cut down like the grass,
And wither as the green herb.
³ Trust in the LORD, and do good;
Dwell in the land, and feed on His faithfulness."

Though people who are not following the plan of God appear to be prospering, the words tells us that there will come a day where they will be cut off, but if we as believers remain faithful to the Lord, He will continue to sustain us, even when things don't appear as we think they should.

The major factor in relinquishing worry is to trust God. We must learn how to trust God with all that is in us and allow Him to be the Sovereign King that He is. Once we do this, we open ourselves up for the many blessings He holds, and give Him total control of our lives, placing us in a position where we never have to worry about anything.

Begin to activate your faith today by making a declaration of faith; renouncing fear, doubt and worry today. Commit to starting a new faith walk and removing all worry from your life!

Application Prayer:

Heavenly Father,

Help me to remove all doubt, all worry and all fear from my life. I know that you are able to do exceedingly and abundantly above all that I may ask or think, and today I commit to putting more trust in You, Your word and Your promises. Help my faith to become stronger and keep my eyes focused, that I won't become distracted by the possessions of those in the world, knowing that my advantage is greater because I live for You.

These things I pray in Jesus' name,

Amen

Pure Joy

Psalm 16:11 NKJV "You will show
me the path of life;
In Your presence is fullness of joy;
At Your right hand are pleasures
forevermore."

Do you know what brings you joy? If your initial thought was something materialistic, my hope is to transform your thinking today. To find joy in things that are materialistic is to find joy in things that are temporary. When I began to think on this more deeply, I began to ponder if the feelings that come with gaining or possessing something temporary were joy at all...the conclusion I came to was that materialistic things make us happy, but could never bring us joy.

You may ask, what is the difference between happiness and joy? Well, happiness is something that is temporary, where joy is unconditional and eternal. Joy comes through Jesus Christ and His love. To be happy is

71

to have temporary feelings that are circumstantial, to be joyful is to have positive feelings no matter the circumstance. For example, if one has a full bank account and is able to purchase anything they set their eyes on, they may be happy. This same person may be discouraged and may even become depressed if they lose all of that money and the possessions as well. A person who has joy would be able to think positive whether their account is empty or full, whether they gain many possessions or not. The same is with someone who encounters challenging situations- when someone has the joy of the Lord, they are able to praise God even in the midst of a tragic situation.

As believers in Christ, the joy of the Lord is a source of strength in any challenging situation (Nehemiah 8:10). Having joy in the midst of a storm is also the root of faith and perseverance in trying circumstances (James 1:2).

A simple instruction to finding joy is to get into the presence of God. The word tells us in Psalm 16:11 that in the presence of the Lord there is *"fullness of joy; at thy right hand there are pleasures for evermore."* When we cast all of our cares on the Lord, we are then in position to experience the fullness of His joy. Along with this joy comes feelings of peace and assurance that we sometimes do not even understand ourselves.

We must also remember that when we cast our cares on Christ to *LEAVE THEM THERE*! One of the biggest mistakes a believer can make is to lay our issues at the alter and pick them back up. Not only does this show a lacking in faith, but it also brings on unnecessary stress when we could be experiencing the joy and peace of God while He solves all of our problems.

Another way that we may find joy is to do things that brings joy to others. Serving in a way that Christ expects can bring joy to the lives of many. From saying something encouraging to someone, to random acts of kindness or even a simple smile, these things can bring joy to the life of someone who may be having a difficult time more than you may ever know.

What things can you release in order to fully experience the joy of the Lord? How can you spread the joy of the Lord to others? Take this time to reflect and write down things that need to be given to God so that you can experience the fullness of His joy and write down ways that you can share the joy of the Lord with others.

Application Prayer:

Heavenly Father,

I come asking that You will fill me with Your joy. Teach me how to abide in Your presence in times of difficulty, that I may experience the fullness of Your joy in the midst of difficult situations. I pray the You would teach me how to share Your joy with others in a manner that would change their life, and inspire them to share Your joy with others. I thank You for every moment that I have been able to experience Your joy already, and pray that there are many joy filled days to come.

In Jesus' name, Amen.

Our Desires, His desires

Psalm 37:4 KJV

"Delight thyself also in the Lord: and he shall give thee the desires of thine heart."

Have you ever wondered what God's plan was for your life? For some of us, there have been many times where we have found ourselves daydreaming, thinking of a prestigious position in the area of your career choice, a husband or wife and children playing outside of an elaborate house with a picket fence…but how often have we taken the time to ask God what His divine plan is for our life? In the word, we see where God tells Jeremiah:

"For I know the plans I have for you," declares the LORD, "plans to prosper you and not to harm you, plans to give you hope and a future." (Jeremiah 29:11 NIV).

The same thing God said to Jeremiah is the same thing that God is speaking to us today. We must make sure we position our ear to hear the plan of God so that we don't move on our own plans and end up in a position of disappointment. God also promises us that when we commit to His way, He will establish our plans (Proverbs 16:3); trusting in the Lord brings forth order in every aspect of our life and gives us clear, sound direction.

The best way to make sure that we are following the plan of God is to ask Him to align the desires of our heart with His. *"When our desires are aligned with the plan of God, we will then desire for His will to be done in our life."* (Apostle Felisha L. Coady). We should make sure that our heart is in the same position the author of Psalm 37:4 was to make sure that our focus is in the right place. Just as the word tell us to make the Kingdom of God our primary focus and everything else will fall into place (Matthew 6:33).

Listening to the voice of God will help us find out what His desires are for us. As we become more and more in tune with Him, our primary desire becomes to

77

please God in a way that our own will is surrendered and we take His will as ours. We will know we are at a place where we have taken His will as our own when we are able to say yes to His instructions without pondering too much on the "what if's" that try to dwell in our mind.

We also have to make sure not to lean to our own understanding. The bible tells us in Proverbs 3:5-6 to:

"⁵Trust in the LORD with all your heart,
And lean not on your own understanding;
⁶ In all your ways acknowledge Him,
And He shall direct your paths."

When we trust in the Lord and allow Him to direct our path rather than leaning to our own understanding, we are always destined to make the right choices and to follow His desires to success. We must always make sure that we place our trust in the Lord regarding our life and future, and our desires for life will become the same as His desires for us.

I challenge you to take some time to listen to the Lord's voice regarding your next steps in life and write down His response. Write down things that will help you follow His perfect plan with ease- this may mean writing down some things you need to let go of or habits you may need to throw away.

Application Prayer:

Father,

Today I pray that You guide my footsteps in Your perfect will. I know You have designed a purpose and plan for my life, and I desire to fulfill it. I pray that You would move anything out of the way that does not align with Your will for me, and help me not to desire things that are not a part of Your plan. Help me to hear Your voice clearly, that I won't follow instructions I thought were from you and end up walking in error, but will be able to discern Your voice and directions clearly.

In Jesus' name,

Amen

Attitude of Gratitude

Ephesians 1:16 NIV

*"I have not stopped giving thanks for
you, remembering you in my
prayers."*

Giving thanks is one of the greatest expressions
we can give to anyone, including the Lord our Father.
When we show expressions of gratitude, we not only
show that the things others do for us matter, but they
themselves matter to us.

Because of the greatness of our God, showing
gratitude can be as surfaced as thanking God for what we
count as the "little things," or as deep as the miracle
stories some of us have to share. Either way, it is great to
give thanks to the Lord not just for the things He has done
for us, but for who He is to us.

One way to show gratitude to the Lord is to offer a
sacrifice of praise to God, even in the midst of situations

that may not feel the best to us. Hebrews 13:15 says:
"By him therefore let us offer the sacrifice of praise to God continually, that is, the fruit of our lips giving thanks to his name."

We must remember that even in times of adversity, God is still awesome and reigns on the throne, watching us every day and gracing us with His goodness. When we have an attitude of gratitude even in the midst of hardships, we are able to experience His joy and peace, and have a great appreciation for His presence even during our trials. This comes through offering a sacrifice of praise to God; it destroys any thought that the enemy would try to plant in our minds of ungratefulness, diminishing the greatness of God in our minds. One of the greatest things we can be thankful for is the fact that even when we are in the middle of our most difficult situations, God is there. He will never leave us nor forsake us (Deuteronomy 31:8)!

It is important that we show appreciation for one another, as we are expected to do for God. Showing appreciation for the things they do for us is an expression of love, as God expects us to. When we show appreciation for others, the things they have done for us or the role they play in our life, it motivates them to express even more love and sacrifice towards us and our needs. So often, we see people who find more fault than they do things to appreciate. This can cause those we love to lose zeal in doing for us or others, and can even be the cause of broken relationships.

We must show our gratitude to God and other not just in words, but in action. Words are important in showing gratitude, but it is our actions that speak even more volumes of our appreciation for those who are important in our life.

Displaying acts of kindness to those who have displayed those acts to us is a great way to show gratitude. Matthew 7:12 tell us to *"do unto others as you would have them do unto you."* If we want others to display appreciation for the things they do for us or the role we play in their life we must do the same.

If we want to continue to experience the blessings of God in their fullness, we must show appreciation for them by offering a sacrifice of praise, and through our actions by helping others and even worshipping God the way He desires to be worshipped, living a lifestyle of holiness. When we live holy, we show our biggest appreciation for God sending His Son, Jesus Christ, to die on the cross for the sins of the world.

How have you shown an attitude of gratitude? Who in your life could you show more appreciation to? How can you show more appreciation for God for His greatness, kindness, and the mercy that He renews in our life every morning?

I encourage you to brainstorm ways to show more appreciation to God for all He has done in your life. Also, think of three people who you may have overlooked or may not have shown as much appreciation to. Write a list for each of them with ten things you are grateful for, and place it in a place that they go often for them to find and read. This may mean writing it on a sticky note and placing it on the steering wheel of your husband or wife's car, or placing it on the mirror in the morning. Sending a card to a friend, a leader, anyone in your life who you feel you have not shown enough gratitude and watch how touching it will be to their life.

Application Prayer:

Heavenly Father,

Give me a heart that shows more appreciation to those who are important to me. Help me to see deep into Your heart, that I may be able to even show a greater appreciation for You, who You are, and all that You are...help me not to focus so much on the faults or flaws of others, but on their efforts to be helpful or show kindness and love towards me. Even with those who it may be most difficult, help me to find the good, the things within them that I can be thankful for.

I thank You for everything You have done for me from waking me up each morning, to sending Your Son to die for me and the sins of the world. Help me to have a greater attitude of gratitude in all things.
In Jesus' name, Amen.

PRIDE- Our Biggest Contender

Proverbs 18:12 ERV

"A proud person will soon be ruined,
but a humble person will be
honored."

Pride is one of the enemy's devices used to cause believers to self-destruct. There are many different forms of pride in operation daily, most of those ways people may not even realize. My prayer is that through this chapter, those ways are revealed and encourage you to self-examine and prepares you to go on a journey of removing all pride from your heart and spirit.

Has anyone ever tried to help you with anything and you found yourself saying "It's okay, I have it?" Perhaps someone has tried to give you something when you were in need and you turned it down…these are simple ways that the spirit of pride can be in operation without us

87

realizing it. When someone makes us an offer, it is better to ask God if it is His will for us to take it rather than completely turning it down; God may have sent that person to be a blessing.

Another form of pride is competing with others. When we find ourselves in competition with others, we lose sight of the vision God has set for us, and even who we are. Competing with other people can send us to a place of idolatry; where we are idolizing ourselves. When we operate in the spirit of pride and find ourselves competing, we place ourselves higher than others and if we are not careful, we can even find ourselves putting us and our desires as equal with God, if not greater. This was the issue that occurred in Heaven with Lucifer. The word of God states in Luke 10:18 that Lucifer fell from Heaven *"like lightning!"* This occurred because Lucifer took on this mindset spoken of in Isaiah chapter 14:

12 How art thou fallen from heaven, O Lucifer, son of the morning! how art thou cut down to the ground, which didst weaken the nations!

13 For thou hast said in thine heart, I will ascend into

heaven, I will exalt my throne above the stars of God: I will sit also upon the mount of the congregation, in the sides of the north:

14 I will ascend above the heights of the clouds; I will be like the most High.

What if Lucifer had decided to continue his work in the Kingdom of God rather than becoming prideful and competing with God? Things would have been so much smoother for him, the angels that began to follow and fell with him, and the scenario in the Garden of Eden would have never taken place. Instead, we see Lucifer bring brought down in verse 15 of that passage where it says:

15 Yet thou shalt be brought down to hell, to the sides of the pit.

Any way, shape or form that we refuse the will of God for our life is operating in the spirit of pride. Rebellion is one of the major attachments to the spirit of pride. If we look at what we just read from the book of Isaiah regarding Lucifer, his prideful spirit caused him to rebel against God, getting him put out of Heaven.

In the book of Proverbs, discussed are seven abominations, things that the Lord hates and despises; the very first of these is "a proud look" (Proverbs 6:17). God does not want us to have a proud appearance before others, but desires us to walk in humility. Even Jesus Christ, who is Lord of Lords made no reputation of himself when he came to earth (Philippians 2:7), but walked in humility, helping everyone that he could, and ministering to those others would have turned away.

If we are operating in sin and refuse to go through the deliverance process, that is the spirit of pride in operation due to the rebelliousness displayed against God's will for us to be free, and us idolizing our fleshly desires so much that we would rather *them* be gratified than God. Operating in the spirit of pride can put us in a place of bondage. As long as we have pride, we are bound to our flesh, a carnal mind and ungodly desires. The God we serve desires for us to be free. He has promised us that the "meek shall inherit the earth" (Matthew 5:5) but that those who are proud will fall (Proverbs 16:18).

When we re-visit some of the situations that occurred in our life, we should ask ourselves: *How could that situation have gone better had the spirit of pride not taken over? What can I do better next time? What signs can I take from previous situations that the spirit of pride is trying to creep into my situation?* If we take the time to reflect on these things, it will assure that we will be alert and ready to counteract any attacks the enemy may try to bring our way.

Reflect on some different situations that have occurred and write down some things you have gathered from those situations as to how to handle the spirit of pride. Also, I encourage you to write down some of the warning signs you have found through your past experiences that the spirit of pride may be trying to creep into a present situation.

Application Prayer:

Father,

I pray that You would keep my heart and mind, that the spirit of pride would not take over in any form. Help me to remain humble in all my ways and be watchful of any way that would become prideful. Help me to be confident in who You made me and what You have called me to do, that the spirit of pride would have no place in my life. I thank You for promising an abundance for me as long as I remain humble, and I trust that as long as pride is not in my spirit, You would never let me fall.

In Jesus' name, Amen!

Choosing Relationships

Amos 3:3 NKJV
Can two walk together, unless they
are agreed?

One of the most difficult things for us to do is to
choose relationships with wisdom. But why? Because we
are fleshly beings who are centered around emotions.
This is why we find ourselves in situations where we
have chosen the wrong type "friends," we find ourselves
in unhealthy relationships, and even find ourselves
desperately holding on to people we know deep inside we
should let go of. "Ungodly covenants are built due to lack
of wisdom." (Apostle Dr. Gail Davis). Our desire to have
our fleshly, emotional needs met often times supersedes
our spiritual needs and ethical beliefs. For example, a
godly woman may find herself in a relationship with a
man who does not desire to have a relationship with God,
but may believe so much that she can change him not to
let him go; only to find in the long run that *she* is
changing or becoming stagnant. This is because she has

laid her ethical belief and biblical teaching to the side that tells her not to be *"unevenly yoked"* (2 Corinthians 6:14), because she so desires that love and affection from that individual.

Another scenario would be someone who has had a close friend since their earlier years of life, but may find later that they are beginning to grow apart due to life changes, changes in standards or beliefs, or even in goals. This type of relationship may be difficult to sever for the same reasons. What do we do in these type situations? We must rely on the love of Christ as a source of strength, and ask for guidance as to where the relationship should go. In some situations, it is obvious as to whether the relationship should end or not, but there are others where it may be difficult to see; in these situations, consulting God is the wisest choice we can make. When we hold steadfast to the love of God, the Holy Spirit will comfort us even when it may be difficult to let go of those we have been attached to.

We must be selective in the people we choose to connect or associate ourselves with. Because God has purpose for each and every one of us, it is important that we are connected to people who will pour into us in a positive manner rather than pour negativity into our life or tear us down. We have to look at both the small pieces as well as the big picture when we choose our friends and relationships. When choosing relationships, some of the questions we should ask ourselves are:

- Does this connection glorify God?
- Are they Kingdom-minded?
- What are their goals?
- Are they capable of pouring into me in a positive manner, or will I be involved in negativity?
- Are they an asset to my life, or will their presence cause conflict?
- What would be the result of this relationship?
- Is this connection beneficial to our future?

These are only a few of the many questions we should ask when connecting with others. Asking these questions will assure that you are properly analyzing the objective of your connection with another individual before it begins. This will also help you determine if you should go forward or not.

When dealing with a significant other, there are other factors that come into play. In addition to the points mentioned above, as you are getting to know an individual who could potentially become a significant other, there should be an even deeper observation of their relationship with Christ. One thing believers should never forget is that a person's love for God should be exceedingly greater than their love for you. If they have not shown that they can love our God, who is their Creator with all their heart, soul and might (Deuteronomy 6:5), how much can they really love us? As I discussed in an earlier chapter, we should love with the heart of God and not our own heart. If a significant other can love with the heart of God, they can love you forever, because God's love is everlasting and they are loving with the heart of God. This means that you should never have to worry about infidelity, mistrust, abuse or any other thing that is not displayed as the love of

God. The bible clearly tells us in 1 Corinthians 13: 4-8 NIV that:

"⁴Love is patient, love is kind. It does not envy, it does not boast, it is not proud. ⁵ It does not dishonor others, it is not self-seeking, it is not easily angered, it keeps no record of wrongs. ⁶ Love does not delight in evil but rejoices with the truth. ⁷ It always protects, always trusts, always hopes, always perseveres.⁸ Love never fails."

When looking at these values, we should ask ourselves in every relationship if they are being displayed. If they are not, then that is a sign that is it not God-ordained and it is in our best interest to let go.

Who are some people who are important to your life? Are they people who are permanently placed, or people who are to serve a temporary purpose? Journal about some people you know are permanent people in your life and why they are most important to you. Then, write a few thank you cards to a few of

those people as a way to show love to them and
appreciation for your relationship with them.

Application Prayer:

Heavenly Father,

*Thank You for providing tools that teach me how to
discern whether opportunities to connect with others are
from You. Help me to discern if connections with others
are permanent or temporary and what the objective of the
connection should be. I pray that you lead and guide
every godly relationship I may have, and that You give me
wisdom on how to grow that relationship in You whether
it is with friends, family or significant others. Help me to
build relationships with others that glorify You and bring
souls to You for the advancement of Your Kingdom,
including business or ministry relationships. Help me to
remember to love others with Your heart, and to display
all of characteristics of love You have defined in Your
word, as You expect others to display to me. Please help
me to let go of connections, friendships and relationships
that are not ordained by You. Break every soul tie that*

may have come from ungodly relationships, that I may be able to walk in freedom and no longer feel connected people of my past. I thank You that Your love never fails and will always be a source I can rely on in every relationship as long as I am obedient to Your instructions regarding my connections with others.

In Jesus' name,

Amen

Restoring Our Heart Condition

Psalm 147:3 NKJV "He heals the brokenhearted...And binds up their wounds."

The heart is a very significant part of the body primarily because the word of God tells us in Proverbs 4:23 that *"out of it flows the issues of life."* This means everything we encounter touches our heart in some form or fashion, and comes out the form of feelings and even actions. Our heart acts as a service center to the rest of our body as well as our spirit. This is why it is important that we follow the word when it tells us to guard our heart (Proverbs 4:23a). There is a reason the bible says *"so a man thinketh in his heart so is he"* (Proverbs 23:7). *Why doesn't the word say so a man thinketh in his mind?* The reason behind this is that when we first encounter something, it first enters our mind. When something enters our mind, it may be easier to get out, but once it

102

penetrates our heart, it becomes a deeper issue. This is why it is extremely important for us to *"cast down imaginations and every high thing that exalts itself against the knowledge of God; and bring every thought into captivity, to the obedience of Christ"* (2 Corinthians 10:5) before our heart is penetrated by the issue and it becomes deeper. If we fail to do this, then thoughts will penetrate our heart to the point that they become a stronghold and are harder to break. Our heart is very sensitive and can easily become contaminated if we are not careful.

It is very important for us to allow God to perform heart surgery on us when we have been wounded. One of the most important reasons why is-when the heart is infected, the body is affected. Think about it, in the natural when one has congestive heart failure, this is a result of the heart not pumping enough blood supply for the other organs. When we look at this same condition in the spiritual, this is like our heart being in such a bad condition that we are not able to effectively minister or spread the love of Christ to others as we should. This can be related to the saying "hurting people hurt people."

When our heart is bitter, we may constantly have a negative attitude and display that to others. Where in the natural, congestive heart failure is not contagious, in the spiritual, this is not the case. If we are not careful, the same attitude we are displaying due to our heart being wounded can be spread to someone else through the things we say or do. This can cause a domino effect to happen in our lives where the spirit of offense becomes in operation, depression and so many other feelings and emotions that could even cause broken relationships.

Taking an even deeper look at Congestive Heart Failure in the natural, one of the things that occurs is that the body tries to compensate for what the heart is not doing, and covers up so well that a person with CHF may not even know they have it until their heart and body has accumulated much damage. How different is this in the spiritual realm? Not much.

There are so many people who walk around in the spirit of offense, who have been hurt or mistreated, who carry issues in their heart but try to cover it up by pretending to be well, pretending that nothing has happened to them, or even operating in the spirit of pride to try to cover up the pain. There are even some people who don't realize that they are wounded because something tragic occurred and they never took the time to sit still long enough to acknowledge the issues. These type people walk around internally bleeding, some running and hiding from their past because they do not want to deal with the issues, others trying to convince themselves that they are healed when they haven't even sought help. This is even the case with many spiritual leaders today....preaching, prophesying, laying hands and even doing deliverance while bleeding inside...all due to a heart condition they have not allowed God to restore.

Besides tragic encounters that cause our heart to become wounded and in bad condition, sin can also put our heart in a bad place. Jeremiah 17:9 tells us that "the heart is deceitful and desperately sick..." Jeremiah then poses a question in the same scripture asking "Who can understand it?"...often times we ask this question ourselves. We will say from our mouth that we know God knows our heart, but at other times we will say that no one understands our agony. God understands every issue of the heart, whether it is something tragic, and even knows the sin that has taken precedence in our heart. This is why He sent Jesus to die on the cross for us, that restoration could take place in our heart.

How do we allow God to restore the condition of our heart? Through the word of God! Hebrews 4:12 tells us *"For the word of God is living and powerful, and sharper than any two-edged sword, piercing even to the division of soul and spirit, and of joints and marrow, and is a discerner of the thoughts and intents of the heart."* When we allow the word of God to penetrate our heart, it begins to cut away and destroy everything that is not like God whether it is the result of ill feelings or sin. This purification process assures us that the wounds will heal properly as God performs surgery on our heart and "binds up the wounds" (Psalm 147:3).

The word promises us that where our flesh and heart may fail us, that God is the strength of our heart and our portion forever (Psalm 73:26); what a wonderful promise! It is such an amazing feeling to know that we have Jesus as the lifeline when everything else fails us. He is near to those who are broken hearted and crushed in spirit, and promises to restore us and has even sent the Holy Spirit to be our comforter through this process.

What areas of your heart are in need of restoration? Think back and journal on issues that have never been resolved that may have your heart bleeding. There may be some people you need to talk to that will help begin the restoration process- after praying for godly wisdom, write the names of those people down and try to connect with them. Be transparent with yourself- if there are any issues in your heart like low self-esteem, depression, anger, etc. write them down and find scriptures associated with those issues to read and meditate on, pray about the issues and allow God to transform your heart. Remember not to be afraid to surrender those issues to God. In the natural often times when people hear that they have to receive surgery they may become fearful, but remember that when God performs surgery, it is always for the better and is beneficial to our heart, mind, body and spirit.

Application Prayer:

Father,

I come surrendering my heart to You...mend every broken place and wounded space and bring it back to full restoration. Touch my mind and remove any negative thought that may try to penetrate my heart or attach itself as a stronghold. I pray that every issue within my heart be resolved that I may walk in perfect health in the natural as well as the spiritual. Lord I trust You, and without fear I am willing to accept the changes that will occur as you transform my heart. I understand that my heart and my flesh may fail me, and believe that You will continue to be my strength and portion forever. I trust You to perform surgery on my heart and mold it until it is pleasing in Your sight. Thank you for thinking enough of me that You would take my heart and make it brand new. In Jesus' name, Amen.

Strive for Holiness: Turning Away From Sin

Acts 3:19 NIV
"Repent, then, and turn to God, so
that your sins may be wiped out, that
times of refreshing may come from the
Lord."

Turning away from sin is one of the wisest decisions we could ever make. This assures that we will secure our place in Heaven with our Father after physical death, in addition to confessing with our mouth and believing in our heart that Christ is our Lord and Savior (Romans 10:9-10). When we make a conscious decision to turn away from sin, we are turning from everything that could bring destruction in our life.

Turning away from sin requires us to turn from our fleshly desires. Why is it so difficult for us to do this? Because evil is always present (Romans 7:21). If we look

110

at all of the days of creation in Genesis chapter 1, we see that God said each and every day was good, except the second day which is the day the firmament was created (Genesis 1:6-8). It is believed that the reasoning behind this is because Satan, the Prince of the Air (Ephesians 2:2) was already in the atmosphere during the time of creation (Pastor Al Mosley). This lets us know that the enemy has been out to take the souls of God's people since the beginning of time, and that this battle between flesh and spirit is constant. As believers in Christ, our responsibility is to keep our body, which is the temple of the Holy Spirit (1 Corinthians 6:19) clean, and to mortify our flesh (Colossians 3:5) that we may be holy and acceptable unto God our Father (Romans 12:1).

When we turn away from sin, we are much better off than we could have ever been. Once we make a decision to be free, it is best to stay free. In the book Matthew, the bible tells us that when we are free, if we do not do what is necessary to stay free, the spirit that was once in us goes and gets seven more spirits and when it returns, the result is that we become worse off than we were before. When we give in to the desires of the enemy, we place ourselves deeper and deeper in bondage. The bible tells us in Galatians 5:1:

"Stand fast therefore in the liberty wherewith Christ hath made us free, and be not entangled again with the yoke of bondage."

When we allow Christ to free us from the chains of sin, we are free indeed (John 8:36)! We do not have to worry about the wages of sin and we take our place as heirs to the Kingdom of God! Christ led captivity captive (Ephesians 4:8) when he shed his blood on the cross for our sins so that we would never have to live our lives in bondage, but can be free in Him.

How can we assure that when we turn away from sin we will stay free? The first step is to stay in the word of God. Psalm 119: 9-12 says:

9 How can a young man cleanse his way?
By taking heed according to Your word.
10 With my whole heart I have sought You;
Oh, let me not wander from Your commandments!
11 Your word I have hidden in my heart,
That I might not sin against You.

112

¹² Blessed are You, O LORD!
Teach me Your statutes.

When we take heed to the word of God, we not only walk in alignment as God expects, but we feed our spirit-man what is necessary for spiritual survival. As we read and meditate on the word, it becomes hidden, even engrafted in our heart so that in times of temptation we are able to see the way of escape God has created for us (1 Corinthians 10:13).

In order to remain focused, we must also *"pray without ceasing"* (1 Thessalonians 5:17). As long as we commune with God and stay in constant communication, we leave no idle time for the enemy to try to have precedence in our life. Prayer strengthens our spirit and takes us higher in God. Along with the armor of God, the word tell us in Ephesians chapter 6 that prayer and supplication will protect us against all principalities, powers, rulers and darkness of this world, as well as all spiritual wickedness in high places (Ephesians 6:12).

Putting on the mind of Christ is extremely important when we are attempting to turn away from sin.

Philippians 2:5 tells us to *"let this mind be in you, which is also in Christ Jesus."* This pertains to anything concerning the Lord our God. When we put on the mind of Christ, the principles given above come naturally; all of them are a never-ending cycle.

What are some struggles with sin you may have and need to break free from? Today, I challenge you to make a checklist of struggles you may have, and begin to thank God in advance for your deliverance. Next, look up scriptures pertaining to those struggles and incorporate them into your prayers as you pray regarding your struggles. Cross off your checklist and even write the date next to it as you watch God work on your spirit. One day, you will have your checklist to look over, how it is all checked off, and a timeline to show where God has brought you from, and where He has taken you to.

Application Prayer:

Father,

I thank You for sending Your son to die on the cross for my sins. Thank You for giving me the opportunity to eternal life and to turn away from sin. I pray for Your

114

strength and guidance as I continue my journey towards spiritual freedom, and pray that You help me remove any spiritual shackles that may hold me in captivity. I know that You are able to break every yoke and sustain me in liberty, therefore I will make a commitment to communing with You daily, without ceasing, meditating on Your word day and night, and being transformed by the renewing of my mind. Help me to take every way of escape You make for me in times of temptation, and to be receptive to people who enter my life and will assist me with spiritual accountability. Again, I give You thanks.

In Jesus' name, Amen.

Accepting the Divine Invitation

Matthew 25:31, 34 KJV
"31 When the Son of man shall come in his glory, and all the holy angels with him, then shall he sit upon the throne of his glory: 34 Then shall the King say unto them on his right hand, Come, ye blessed of my Father, inherit the kingdom prepared for you from the foundation of the world:"

The greatest place ever seen in heaven or on earth is the Kingdom of God. God has given us a divine invitation to dwell in His Kingdom. Do we have a full understanding of what this means for us? Gaining understanding would be one of the wisest decisions we have ever made.

So, what does having a divine invitation to the Kingdom of God mean for us? Firstly, this means that we have a personal, open invitation to the presence of God.

117

In the Old Testament, we see that the priest had to wear certain garments to enter the tabernacle. They also had to continuously wash their hands, and go through different levels before they could even get to the Holy of Holies; they had to be able to get through the inner and outer court alive based on their purity. There were sacrifices that had to be burned and there was even a string tied around the waist of the priest in case of a mishap so that the people could pull them out of the tabernacle if they did not live. When Jesus died on the cross, scripture tells us that the veil between the courts and the Holy of Holies ripped down the middle (Matthew 27:51), giving us personal access to the presence of God! When we enter the presence of God through invitation, we get to experience the fullness of joy (Psalm 16:11)!

Secondly, the divine invitation God has given us has invited us to experience His liberty. 2 Corinthians 3:17 tells us that *"where the Spirit of the Lord is, there is liberty."* Once we accept God's invitation to His presence, we experience freedom in Jesus Christ to break away from any yoke of bondage that would try to keep us captive- whether it be sickness or disease, habits or addictions, depression or oppression. This also is a divine invitation to salvation; we are able to live again through Jesus Christ who shed his blood for the remission of our sins (Matthew 26:28)!

When we accept the divine invitation God has extended to us to dwell in His Kingdom and presence, everything else that God has we are granted access to! His blessing, favor, grace, mercy, protection and so many other things that God has- most of all, his promises! There are many promises the bible speaks of and when we accept the invitation to the Kingdom of God, we accept our heirship, inheriting all of those promises.

We must remember that when we are given the invitation, and we make it to the presence of God, not to return to our old ways, habits or lifestyle. The only reason we should look back is to help lead or guide someone else to the presence of God, who may not know their way.

Another thing we must remember is that there will be times where the enemy will try to stop us from getting to the presence of God. Of course, Satan is upset because he lost his opportunity, therefore him and the angels of

119

darkness will do everything in their power to keep us from making it to the presence of God. The best way to fight this is to allow the word of God to be our map, and worship to be our GPS. Worship will lead us into the presence of God while the word of God makes sure that we are also on the right track and tells us everything we need to know about our journey. When we get into the presence of God, the vehicle, Holy Spirit, will drive us past every roadblock the enemy may try to create, and will even mount us up on wings as eagles (Isaiah 40:31) that we may travel over every one, no matter how big it may appear to be.

But where does wisdom come in to play? Wisdom is the key! In order for us to go anywhere, we must use godly wisdom to decide that it is best for us in the first place. God will not force us to take His invitation, it is up to us to use the wisdom He has placed in us to do what is best for our spirit- to allow the Holy Spirit to drive us, to allow worship to lead us, to allow the word of God to direct us with detail, and to allow God to transform us, preparing us to make our entrance into His presence and Kingdom.

Have you accepted the invitation from Christ? The invitation to His presence, His peace, and all that He has to offer? What things are holding you back? I challenge you today to make the wisest decision you can make and accept the invitation to make Christ your Lord and Savior and even if you have, to do it all over again as a rededication and commitment to be joined in heirship with Him. Reflect on ways that you have tried to drive yourself and may have made the wrong decision, how you may have allowed someone else to be your GPS or provide you with a map other than worship or the word and how it may have taken you off course…what effects did it have on your life? How can you assure that you will remain on the right track so that it doesn't occur again?

Accept the invitation to God, enter into His presence and He will help guide you when opportunity knocks, He will help you remove all negativity from your life, be who He has destined you to be and embrace the wonderful, incredible person that you are. He will help you grow in integrity and faithfulness, forgive and forget, wisely choose relationships, experience pure joy and even teach you how to increase in faith rather than worrying. When you accept His invitation, God can restore your heart condition, assist you in turning from sin and dealing with pride, align the desires of your heart with his, grow up and most of all-WISE UP!

Application Prayer:

Lord,

I thank You for giving me a divine invitation to Your presence, to liberty and salvation and to Your promises. Today I have decided to make the wisest decision I can make and dedicate myself to You as my Lord and personal Savior. I pray that You would help me to use worship as my GPS, that would guide me into Your presence even in stormy seasons in my life, and that Your word will be my map, giving me in depth details of Your expectations and directions for my life journey. I pray that Your Holy Spirit will be the vehicle that drives me to Your presence at all times, that I will always use the key of wisdom You have placed inside of me. Help me to always look past the road blocks the enemy may try to put in my way, that I may press towards the mark for prize of the high calling in You, reaching Your presence....Your Kingdom.

In the mighty name of Jesus, Amen!

About the Author

Pastor Chenelle Coleman-Price resides as Assistant Pastor of True Divine Kingdom Ministries in Cincinnati, Ohio. She is a woman of God known for her gifts not only in Cincinnati, but in various cities.

She has taught classes to equip Armorbearors for ministry, worked with children and youth ministries for over 10 years, served as a worship leader at True Divine Kingdom Ministries and participated in various evangelism and outreach projects. She attended Cincinnati Christian University, where she received ministerial and biblical training and received her bachelor's degree at Union Institute & University, a private college, in Early Childhood Education. She is also an elementary school teacher and the co-owner of ELAB Visionary Productions, a graphic and web-design company.

Although she has been faced with many obstacles in her years of ministry, Pastor Chenelle has stood on her favorite scripture, which still encourages her to go forward today:

"We are troubled on every side, yet not distressed; we are perplexed, but not in despair; Persecuted, but not forsaken; cast down, but not destroyed."

~ 2 Corinthians 4:8

For live updates, purchases and more information on the

Wise Up Challenge, go to:

www.wiseupchallenge.com

or check out our Facebook page:

Wise Up Challenge